The Size of Dark Cherries

poems by

Lisa Olsson

Finishing Line Press
Georgetown, Kentucky

The Size of Dark Cherries

For my children
Ian and Em

ACKNOWLEDGMENTS

With thanks to the editors who published the following poems:

Lumina, Vol XVIII, "Pushing Trees"
The Westchester Review, Volume 9, "New York Divorce"

Thanks and love to the teachers at the Hudson Valley Writers' Center and
my Monday night poetry group for all the support and guidance that has
made my poetry journey possible.

Publisher: Leah Huete de Maines
Editor: Christen Kincaid
Cover Art: Lisa Olsson
Author Photo: Bob Plotkin
Cover Design: Elizabeth Maines McCleavy

Order online: www.finishinglinepress.com
also available on amazon.com

Author inquiries and mail orders:
Finishing Line Press
PO Box 1626
Georgetown, Kentucky 40324
USA

Contents

Dwarf Lilac

The globe of petals
is flattened to a halo on the ground
like a recent memory
flavored with imagined scent
I'm not ready to sweep

Last Spring

it rained water
milkweed
petals catkins

you came home
got your things

it rained stones
the size of
dark cherries

Pushing Trees

The heart of Sunday—after church
dinner in the oven, no thought
of Monday—we're out with the dogs.
I'm a girl in the woods
Dad pushes down dead trees—
my coat's particular blue, its nubs
and sculpted rose buttons, the satin lining—
I don't love like that anymore.

Compost

I push aside the curtain
of weeping willow, pry
the cover and dump the pail

look in the dark hole
where worms work
without stopping—

the persistent night
that heals our wounds.

A strawberry sepal sits
on the rot pile—I picture
the bright skin and smile
of my daughter eating
shortcake last Sunday,
my joy red.

I Know They'll Soon Cease to Walk the Rail

Barefoot and
singing, their breath
against the bigger
breath of wind
the girls walk
on the split rail fence
leap across the gaps
post to post
arms out as if
on a high wire
between city towers.
In my chair
on the sand
reading, watching
occasionally
the wind blows
away their voices
except when they
turn their heads
in my direction.

Remnant

Smoke above the toaster.
I put your flannel shirt on
like the dog who pulls my clothes
off hangers and drags them to her bed
when I'm gone. The shirt is XXL
like everything you do.
That's what scares me.

This is not an empty nester poem.
It's a mother's love poem.
A barking for intercession.
I am the pilgrim, lips to the reliquary
the woman reaching for the hem.
If I only touch his cloak I will be healed.
I am the mother clipping a lock
of my baby's hair, stowing it
in a tin to keep him safe.

New York Divorce

O my pink baby, caught in churn of Hell
Gate stink, jostle in the ebb tide sweep, grab
onto splintered timbers—you can't swim yet—
the jutted rocks fray your puckered fingers.
Among ballooning bags in lilting bilge
your bobblehead oddly fits, another
left over butt flicked into scalloped waves.
We were once your Ursa Major, Pleiades,
you looked up to us and charted journeys,
our high clear eyes the gauge of just how far
you could crawl, infant genius voyager.
But now we are your Scylla and Charybdis.
Steer close to the nasty heads with stiff teeth,
my love, avoid the suck of black water.

Thanksgiving Weekend

I wake up with the word gelatinous in my mouth.
I am divided between overhearing and having a conversation.
I nestle with strangers in Orchestra Row D of the Golden.
I laugh how husband and kids became mine after such refusal.
I hear a glass of wine clock over, people eating elbow to elbow.
I feel the sisters' rancor—one drinks, the curtain falls.
I eat truffle mousse with brandy aspic on toasted baguette.
I stall in the other room, hear my name, rehearse a smile.
I see rows of miniature seats filled with miniature people.
I am pinned on the couch by a lapcat that combs my nose.
I am restless to give everything away.

Side Door

Distressed, as if attacked with a chain when I was a teen—
gouged, grime sheathed, hair stuck on the dirt flecked edge, it
stays closed with a hook and eye latch. One pane missing, a piece
of particle board screwed over the opening. On the side of the
house—seen only by them when they let the feral cat slip in or
fill the birdfeeder. It opens and shuts and makes me mad—they
have the money to buy a new door. I know, the depression,
they're lucky to have a door, a house, a home—it's good enough.
I was born into my parents' past—tight shoes, sleeping on shelves
in the barn, Olaug's homemade bread, Aunt Anna upstairs in
her house dress, darned wool and virginity, great grandma on
a kitchen stool ruling with her cane. I can bang this door, but
how to continue—rip it off, cart it to the dump, demolish the
whole house, I think, as I'm taking the garbage out because Dad's
gone now. Then I see my hand on the knob—veins prominent
like mom's—I know she's up in the kitchen, but I hear her voice
spooning mine—*it's a good old wooden door.*

Visit

39 cents written in pencil
on the cardboard lid
of the Shiny Bright box.
I take out one at a time
welcome the sadness
of you so near
invite you to stay
while I put them on the tree
as you once did.
Tiny glass globes
metallic blue and green
your favorite colors splotched now
with black explosions of corrosion
no longer pretty.

Aunt Edie

A cord from behind her ear down the V neck
of her button-down dress. Hearing loss from scarlet fever.

Waited for a ride to church in the dirt driveway
next to the row of snowball hydrangeas, cream colored

folded dollar bill in hand, a tissue in the sleeve
stiff pocketbook hanging from a wrist.

Evenings warbling Holy, Holy, Holy at the upright.
Silhouette against white lace curtains.

I'm too tall. But Frank answered her ad
in the Miss Lonelyhearts column.

A widower with no children, they married
had two girls, then he died young.

My Grandma—Aunt Edie to the extended family.
Always willing to set an extra place. *I'll get it.*

Darned socks. Wore rummage sale dresses.
Always ready to iron and mend for Mrs. Brinkmeyer.

Scrape the burn off the toast. Knitted mittens for me
fed unshelled peanuts to squirrels by hand.

Made vegetarian steaks with a fake bone during The War
raised her sister's kids, went to church. Never drove.

Came to live with us. Slept in my room
in my sister's old bed. Woke me one night crying

patting my bed, trying to find her bed
without turning on the light. *Where am I?*

Moulting season

It's August 18, my father's birthday—he'd be a hundred and one.
I mourn my loss but am no longer sad as I stoop

to pick up another feather lost by the Osprey and Heron—
too many to count on the driveway, the path to the beach

all white, all gray, black tipped, striped, and spotted.
I will stand them in a glass like my grandmother did.

On the Front Stoop

A screech and diagonal
scatter through trees.
There are my crows, she says.
It sounded like eagle
but red tail, broad wing—hawk.
Our heads lean back in unison
as we watch them ascend,
join a column soaring
in gear motion, clockwise
and counterclockwise
drawn up into the white
sky. I love her even though
she is not the mother I knew
the one who put out
chicken fat for the crows.
I sit with her on the stoop.
They come every day.
I count, starting from the nearest.
Eleven, then more, my eyes
struggle to track as they diminish
to dark specks on invisible dials.
Every day. At the same time.

Snowbed

Done, unable to sleep
I reach for the book
about the man
the woman going
home or leaving.

Retrieval.

Feathers and stones
brought back, lined
up on the sill
away from their beds.

Lost.

When I was twelve
I'd go outside
and lie down
after the snow stopped.

The flat black sky
over my snow hollow
and mom yelling
under the cone of yellow

on the stoop
Don't fall asleep
out there—you
might never wake up.

Company

As the youngest it was her job
to walk to the chicken farm
down Covington Street
past the Whitman house
on Sundays if company came.

She would pick at the fence
eyes on Mr Wiggins' bloody apron
as he took the soft dollar
and reached the brown sack
heavy and scrunched at the top
toward her small hand.

She Who Was My Mother

1

Your night fall
splayed the bookcase

confused the nerves
changed you into

a weird child
stole the secrets

from your eyes
made you believe

that news stories
are your stories

2

I usurp garden
oven car

pull socks on
empty the bowl

am rewarded with
feelings of grandeur

as if I
lay before you

a fire opal
set in gold

3

in their slippers
robes held closed

neighbors come out
into night cold

under sterile font
of winter sky

to the sidewalk
across the street

to watch your wall
and rafters burn

black against orange
a writhing tiger

I Guess She Had Always Lied

You, slick in senility
speak falsehoods with authority
visited your friend last week
are sore from weeding
just had one glass of wine.

Why would I have disbelieved
during your middle age
that you stood on one foot
for a minute every day—
that you had balance under control?

Fleck of Glitter

Why didn't he sign?
The pen inert in his hand.
He couldn't choose to go
to screen test, to Hollywood
to stardom, to fame.

He crooned on Arthur Godfrey
won the Catskills talent show
snagged a part in "Arms and the Girl"
belted many a forte "Figaro"
from atop the outdoor stair.

Did he even have a shot—
do we want to know?
When he tells it after dinner
family all around, he gives
a dramatic pause as the candle
wavers, haloing the head
of our king of possibility.

Looking For That Selfie

Scrolling through photos on my phone

I see my father on his bed, his mouth open.

How death becomes part of life again.

The Way to Kill a Cat

I'm happier when ideas come.
I've been hungry lately.

The way to kill a cat mercifully
is to take it up to 30,000 feet

in an open cockpit plane
without an oxygen mask.

The cat breathes the thinning air
goes unconscious unconsciously.

There is no pain, no awareness.
My father told me this many times.

Grieving Shawl

All five of us hiked
that day in January
after my father died.

Halfway up Storm King
I thought of his story
crossing the Atlantic
after the war.

Seas were rough
he wasn't seasick
something bothered him
I couldn't recall.

The Hudson below
Breakneck Ridge
on the other side.
We stared across.

I remembered—it wasn't
a story, but a passage
in his war journal.
He had hoped to be home
by Christmas, but was lucky
to be coming home
without a scratch.
Hundreds on board
were wounded, missing
legs, arms, eyes.

I felt something
folding around me
arms and a shawl
*the one my mother
knit last winter,* she said
*with all my favorite colors.
You need it now.*

O Father

You gave me a river, current fierce
a barn, pitchfork and hoe.
You gave me a house. You sang.
You gave me a skiff and oars.

The wind its needling teeth.
The oak its dreaded sway.
You gave me a book and fire.
You sharpened my saw.

You gave me a dahlia, symmetry
my eyes, first light, the moon,
a strawberry field sopped with dew
a grape, its whitish bloom.

O father, give me more
give me the sand, its buried stone.
Give me a magnolia, cups upturned
a bench, a path, a broom.

Lisa Olsson's poems have been published in *Ekphrasis, The Westchester Review, BigCity Lit, Lumina, Salt, Ginosko* among others. She was a winner in the Hudson Valley Writers' Center Poetry in the Pavement competition. She is a cellist and abstract painter. She plays in the Yonkers Philharmonic, Westchester Chamber Soloists and Kort String Quartet. Her art has been shown at The Blue Door, Upstream, and East End Arts galleries. She lives in Dobbs Ferry, New York.

www.ingramcontent.com/pod-product-compliance
Lightning Source LLC
Chambersburg PA
CBHW022108080426
42734CB00009B/1511